Condoleezza Rice

by Corinne J. Naden and Rose Blue

Chicago, Illinois

© 2006 Raintree
Published by Raintree, a division of Reed Elsevier, Inc.
Chicago, Illinois
Customer Service: 888-363-4266
Visit our website at www.raintreelibrary.com

For information, address the publisher:
Raintree, 100 N. LaSalle, Suite 1200, Chicago, IL 60602

Printed and bound in China by South China Printing Company.
10 09 08 07 06
10 9 8 7 6 5 4 3 2 1

Library of Congress Cataloging-in-Publication Data:

Naden, Corinne J.
    Condoleezza Rice / Corinne J. Naden and Rose Blue.
        p. cm. -- (African-American biographies)
    Includes bibliographical references and index.
    ISBN 1-4109-1039-3 (hc) 1-4109-1123-3 (pb)
    1. Rice, Condoleezza, 1954---Juvenile literature. 2. National Security
Council (U.S.)--Biography--Juvenile literature. 3. African American women
educators--Biography--Juvenile literature. 4. Presidents--United
States--Staff--Biography. I. Blue, Rose. II. Title. III. Series.
    UA23.15.R53N33 2005
    355'.033073'092--dc22

                            2005005098

Acknowledgments
The publisher would like to thank the following for permission to reproduce photographs:
pp. 4, 36, 40, 77, 50, 56 Corbis/Reuters; p.8 Popperfoto; pp.11, 13, 16, 18 Corbis/Bettman; p.17 Corbis/Kevin Fleming; pp.22, 27 Penrose Library Special Collections & Archives, University of Denver; p. 24 University of Denver; p.29 Harcourt Education, ltd.; pp.30, 33, 40 Associated Press; p.34 Alamy/Stephen Saks Photography; p.41 Rex Features; p.44 Getty Images/AFP; p.49 Corbis/Bob Krist; p.52 Corbis/Reuters/Molly Riley; p.54 Corbis/Jason Reed; p.58 Corbis/Brooks Craft

Cover photograph: Getty Images News/David McNew

Every effort has been made to contact copyright holders of any material reproduced in this book. Any omissions will be rectified in subsequent printings if notice is given to the publisher

Some words are shown in bold, **like this.** You can find out what they mean by looking in the Glossary.

Contents

Secretary of State Condoleezza Rice is a woman of many interests and talents.

Introduction:
A Woman of Many Talents

Condoleezza Rice is the secretary of state to George W. Bush, the president of the United States. She gives President Bush advice about matters that concern foreign countries. When it comes to such matters, she is the person the president trusts most. Prior to being appointed secretary of state, Rice was the first female and first African-American national security **advisor**.

As secretary of state, Condoleezza needs to be both self-confident and tough. She must keep up-to-date on military affairs all over the world. She must keep the president informed about dangers to the United States. She must understand how foreign governments work to help stop problems before they begin. She must be able to talk seriously but fairly to people from any country. She must be able to think on her feet. It is a very demanding job that keeps Rice at her office in the White House for long hours.

Condoleezza Rice is a woman of many gifts and accomplishments. She is a talented musician and speaks Russian **fluently**. Experts say she will be around Washington, D.C. for a long time to come.

Rice has been interested in how government and politics work ever since she was a young girl. But she is interested in other things, too. When she first met George W. Bush, she impressed the future president with her stories about baseball great Willie Mays. Condoleezza's mother taught Mays when he was a student back in Birmingham, Alabama, so she had many stories to tell.

Rice also has a great love of football. At one time, it was her dream to become head of the National Football League.

In Her Own Words

I want to thank the members of my family and my friends who are here–a number are here from Birmingham, Alabama, and they represent generations of Rices and Rays, who believed that a day like this might somehow be possible.

I'm honored by your confidence in me, Mr. President, and I'm deeply grateful for the opportunity you've given me to serve as this country's 66th Secretary of State...

...Now it's time to build on those achievments to make the world safer and even more free. We must use American diplomacy to help create a balance of power that favors freedom. The time for diplomacy is now. Standing for the cause of liberty is as old as our country itself. Indeed, it was our very first Secretary of State, Thomas Jefferson, who said "The God who gave us life, gave us liberty at the same time." ... Our founders realized that they, like all human beings, were flawed creatures, and that any government created by man would not be perfect. Even the great authors of our liberty sometimes fell short of their ideals—even Thomas Jefferson, himself...

...The enduring principles enshrined in our Constitution made it possible for impatient patriots like Frederick Douglass, and Abraham Lincoln, and Martin Luther King to move us ever closer to our founding ideals.

Condoleezza Rice speaking at her swearing in as secretary of state, January, 2005.

Birmingham, Alabama as it looked when Condoleezza Rice was growing up there in the 1950s.

Chapter 1:
With Sweetness

Condoleezza–called "Condi" by her friends–was born on November 14, 1954, in Birmingham, Alabama. Located deep in a southern state, Condi's home town was in the news a lot during her childhood. In this city racial hatred and segregation divided the population. Whites and African Americans stood against each other. Many southern white people believed African Americans were not as good as white people. Condi's parents were determined to raise a daughter who would overcome these challenges. Her mother, Angelena Ray Rice, was a serious piano student. She taught music and science in a suburb of Birmingham, Alabama. She gave Condoleezza her name which comes from a musical term–*con dolcezza*–meaning "with sweetness." Condoleezza's father, John Wesley Rice, was a minister, high school teacher, and head basketball coach. Condoleezza's father called her "Little Star."

Condoleezza grew up among stable, church-going, southern black families who had enough money to live comfortable lives. They were educated people who did well, and they expected their children to be the same. But in Birmingham black people and white people could not eat in the same restaurants, drink from the same drinking fountains, or learn in the same schools. In the 1950s and 1960s, Birmingham became an important part of the **civil rights movement**. Leaders like Dr. Martin Luther King Jr. organized may protests and boycotts in Birmingham to try to convince the United States government to create laws that gave black people the rights they deserved as American citizens.

Education was also a problem in Birmingham. Black students and white students were forced to attend separate schools. By law, these schools were required to be equal.

But the schools were not equal. Schools for black students, especially in the South, were often overcrowded, run-down, and did not have enough money for repairs or supplies. Because there weren't many schools for black children, students often had to travel long distances to attend. White schools, on the other hand, had plenty of money, good supplies, and were usually in much better condition. There were also more of them, so students did not have to travel as far to get to them.

The 1954 case Brown v. Board of Education ended racial segregation in public schools.

Organizations such as the National Association for the Advancement of Colored People (NAACP), had tried for years to desegregate American schools. In the early 1950s, people in several states, including Kansas, brought the issue of school desegregation before the Supreme Court, the most powerful court in the United States. The case became known as *Brown v. Board of Education of Topeka, Kansas.*

Oliver Brown was the father of Linda Brown, a seven-year-old African-American girl who had to travel over an hour each morning, though dangerous areas, just to get to school. There was a school for white children just seven blocks from her house. Linda's father thought she should be able to go there. Brown sued the board for his daughter's right to do so.

In 1954, just six months before Condoleezza was born, the Supreme Court decided that the segregation of public schools was unconstitutional. In other words, school segregation was against the law. The Supreme Court judges–called justices–decided that all children, no matter what their race, deserved the chance to get a good education and that segregation took that chance away. It was many years before public schools became desegregated, so Condoleezza went to a **segregated** school in Birmingham.

Condoleezza's parents knew that with all of the challenges facing African Americans, Condoleezza had to work to be twice as

Thurgood Marshall

Thurgood Marshall was the lawyer who, in the 1954 case of Brown v. Board of Education, convinced the Supreme Court that segregated public schools were unconstitutional. Thirteen years later he became the first African-American Supreme Court justice.

Marshall was born in Baltimore Maryland in 1908. He was named after his grandfather who had been a slave. Marshall attended an all-black high school, and graduated from college at the top of his class. He wanted to go to the University of Maryland for law school, but when he applied, they rejected him because he was black. He went instead to Howard University, an all-black college, and graduated first in his class.

In 1963 Marshall became a lawyer for the National Association for the Advancement of Colored People (NAACP). The NAACP was very active in making sure that black people got the rights the deserved according to the law. It was during his time with the NAACP that Marshall worked to end segregation in different areas of American life. In Texas, he won a case that allowed black people to vote. In another case, he convinced the judges that law schools in Texas and Oklahoma should be integrated. And in 1954, he won Brown v. Board of Education.

In 1965 President Lyndon B. Johnson appointed Marshall to the Supreme Court of the United States. He served on the Court until 1991. Marshall died in 1993.

good as everyone around her. They knew that someday the rich learning experieces they provided for her would allow her to compete with, and eventually out-achieve her white peers. In this way, they hoped to protect their daughter from the limits of **racism**.

Condoleezza took ballet lessons and learned to speak French and Spanish. She took piano lessons, and her mother enrolled her in a music school for black students. There Condoleezza also studied flute and violin. One day when Condi was a little girl, she went shopping with her mother. She found a dress that she wanted to try on. She asked the salesperson where the fitting room was. The salesperson pointed to a storage room. Only white people were allowed to try on clothes in the fitting room. African Americans had to use the storage room.

Condi's mother objected. She did not want her daughter to be treated differently because of the color of her skin. It was humiliating to have to try on clothes in a storage room. She told the salesperson that they would go somewhere else to buy Condi a new dress. The salesperson did not want to lose the sale. She showed Condi where the fitting rooms were, but she stood just outside to make sure no one else saw what happened.

Angelena Rice taught her daughter how to stand up for herself with grace and dignity.

"Grandaddy" Rice

Understanding the importance of education is part of Condoleezza Rice's heritage. Her father's father, John Rice, Jr., was the son of farmers in Alabama who had never gone to school, but his mother could read and write. John could read and write, too but he wanted a formal education. In 1918, when he was old enough, Rice Jr. decided to leave the family farm and go to college.

At the time, it was not easy for a black man to get an education. But John heard about Stillman College in Tuscaloosa, Alabama. It was founded by white Presbyterian ministers in 1874 to train black men 'to' become ministers. So John saved his money and went to school.

At the end of the first year, John was out of money. When he asked his schoolmates how they were able to afford college, they told him that Stillman would pay for his education if he became a Presbyterian minister. And that is just what he did. When he graduated, he became a minister and spent the rest of his life trying to help other young black people get an education.

Condoleezza's father also had a great influence on her early learning. He taught her that with education, anything is possible. He spent Sunday afternoons teaching his daughter to love football. Condoleezza's father worked in the athletic department at a local black high school as an assistant football coach. He was also a former football player, so he had a lot to teach his daughter. As an adult, Condoleezza once joked that once her father realized he wasn't having a son he focused his intense love for sports on her.

The site of the 1963 Birmingham church bombing.

Condoleezza and her father also had important discussions about things going on in the daily news. And in Birmingham in the 1960s, there was a lot to talk about.

In September 1963, Condoleezza was only a few miles away from 16th Street Baptist Church when it was bombed. It was Sunday morning and the church was crowded with people going to services. The blast blew a hole in the side of the church where children were in Sunday school. Four black girls, one age 11 and the other three

Today, the 16th Street Baptist Church looks quite different than it did after the September 15, 1963 bombing. Each year on the aniversary of the bombing the church bells ring in memory of the four girls killed in the blast.

age 14, were killed. The 11-year-old, Denise McNair, had been Condoleezza's friend since kindergarten. Condoleezza attended the girls' funeral as did more than 8,000 people, both black and white. Martin Luther King, Jr. spoke at the funeral. Condi remembered the day for the rest of her life. As an adult looking back on the experience, she said, "I remember more than anything the coffins, the small coffins. And the sense that Birmingham wasn't a very safe place."

These children are being arrested after participating in a peaceful march for civil rights.

The 16th Street Baptist Church had been bombed by members of the Ku Klux Klan, a group of white people who terrorized African Americans and who did not like the progress the **civil rights movement** was making. The church had been a meeting place for people involved in the civil rights movement. Rallies with large numbers of people happened there.

The church bombing was not the only violent reaction to the civil rights movement in Birmingham that year. At night groups of white men ran through black neighborhoods setting fires. Condoleezza's father and other men in her neighborhood protected their families by standing watch with guns. Birmingham schoolchildren marched peacefully in the streets to call for **integrated** schools, but city officials turned fire hoses and police dogs on them to stop the march.

Condoleezza's parents wanted the fight for civil rights to succeed, but they did not think children should be involved. Condoleezza's father wanted her to understand what was happening so he took her to watch some of the demonstrations, but kept her at a safe distance.

When school was out for the summer, Condoleezza and her parents often traveled to Denver, Colorado. Her parents were working on their master's degrees at the University of Denver. This was a long way from Birmingham, Alabama. Because of the color of their skin, the Rices were not allowed to attend graduate school at the University of Alabama. To give Condoleezza something to do while they were in class, they sent her to the ice rink to learn figure skating.

Condoleezza loved to skate. Her years of ballet lessons made her a graceful skater, and she enjoyed being on the ice. When she improved, she entered some skating contests. Although she never really became good enough to compete at a high level, as an adult, she still loves figure skating.

One summer, before going to Denver, the family went to Washington, D.C. Condi was 10 years old when she stood outside the White House. She told her father that although she could not go to the White House then because of the color of her skin, someday she would be in that house.

A new experience

In 1965 Condoleezza's family moved to Tuscaloosa, Alabama, about 60 miles from Birmingham. Her father got an important new job at Stillman College, an historically black university, where her grandfather had been a student.

After three years, the Rice family moved again, this time to Colorado, permanently. Condoleezza's father took a new job at the University of Denver. It was a very big change for the family. For one thing, Denver got about 60 inches of snow every year. That was quite a difference from the hot and humid climate of Alabama. And for Condoleezza, who was now 13, it meant going to an **integrated** school for the first time.

The Klu Klux Klan

In 1866 former Southern Civil War veterans in Tennessee formed the Klu Klux Klan. The Klan started as a social club, but soon its members began harassing, even killing, blacks. In 1868 the Klan killed nearly 1,000 people in Louisiana alone. In the 1920s, when more and more immigrants were coming to the United States, the Klan became popular again. They elected their members to political office and enforced segregation in some parts of the South. The Klan continues to exist today, although it is not as powerful as it once was.

Condoleezza's parents taught her to be twice as good as everyone else so that she could succeed at a time when African-Americans were considered by many to be inferior to whites.

Chapter 2:
Careful Steps to a Career

Condoleezza enrolled in St. Mary's Academy, an all-female, private, integrated Catholic school. It was small, strict, and safe. Condoleezza did very well in her new school. Besides her class studies and figure skating lessons, she learned to play tennis. Her family even bought a grand piano so that she could continue to practice at home.

Because she was such a good student, it was quite a shock to young Condoleezza when she received a lower than average score on a standardized test and was told she was "not college material." But this did not discourage Condoleezza or her parents. Her mother told her to ignore the remark and concentrate on her studies.

Condoleezza concentrated so well at St. Mary's that she completed all the requirements for graduation by the end of her junior year. Her parents thought this was a wonderful opportunity

The University of Denver where Rice's father taught and Rice attended college.

for their daughter. They thought she should leave St. Mary's at the end of her junior year and enroll at the University of Denver.

Condoleezza did not usually disagree with her parents, but this time she did. She wanted to enjoy her last year in high school and attend graduation with her classmates. She had worked for it. She and her parents figured out a way for Condoleezza to finish high school and begin college at the same time.

For the next year, Condoleezza kept an amazing schedule. She took figure skating lessons before the sun came up. Then she had two morning classes at the university and a full afternoon of classes at St. Mary's. In her spare time, she entered and won a piano competition for young people. She went to her senior prom and attended her high school graduation. She was 16 years old when she got her high school diploma, two years younger than most high school graduates.

The first college class that Condoleezza took pushed her into a grown-up world. Her professor presented a theory that said people from Africa, and African Americans, were not as smart or cultured as white people. Condi's parents had taught her to believe she could be anything she wanted to be. She challenged the professor and said the theory was not true. "I am the one who speaks French," she said boldly. "I am the one who plays Beethoven. I am better at your **culture** than you are!" Condi understood the lesson her parents had been teaching her all her life. **Culture** can be taught and it has nothing to do with race. She was only 15 years old, but she had courage to stand up to a college professor.

The career decision

Condoleezza began attending the University of Denver full time in 1970 with a major in music. However, she did not plan on completing her college education there. At the time, there was no better music school than the famous Julliard School of Music in New York City. She wanted to transfer there, but her father would not allow it. He wanted Condoleezza to get more than just an education in music. If she graduated from Julliard and was not good enough to perform professionally, or if she changed her mind, she would not be prepared for another career.

A short time later, when she attended the Aspen Music Festival in Aspen, Colorado, she met 11-year-olds who were already better musicians that she was. She was glad she'd stayed at the University of Denver.

Although Condoleezza knew that she would not continue to make music her major course of study, she did not know what else to choose. She thought about a number of fields, but nothing seemed right. Then one day she walked into a class that changed everything. The course was about international **politics** and the professor was Josef Korbel.

Josef Korbel

Condoleezza Rice says that her college professor, Josef Korbel, steered her toward a career in international politics. Korbel was from Moravia, now part of the Czech Republic. He moved to the Czech capital of Prague in 1928, where he met and married his high school sweetheart.

In 1933 Adolf Hitler took over Germany and began to kill many people in Europe, especially those who were Jewish. Korbel was Jewish, and he knew that he must take his family from Czechoslovakia. They fled to Yugoslavia one dark night in 1938. But that was not safe either. Again they fled, this time to Greece.

Hitler and his armies were defeated in 1945. Korbel then became the Czechoslovakian **ambassador** to Yugoslavia. Three years later, Korbel moved his family to the United States. There were people in Yugoslavia who wanted him dead.

Once he was safely in the U.S, Korbel was hired by the University of Denver to teach international relations. Condoleezza Rice was in his class, which had a huge influence on her.

Condoleezza also met Korbel's oldest daughter, Madeleine. Later, as Madeleine Korbel Albright, she would also make a name for herself in the U.S. government. She was named U.S. Ambassador to the United Nations in 1992. And in 1997, she became the first woman to act as U.S. Secretary of State. She was appointed by President Bill Clinton. In 2005 Rice became the second woman to hold this position.

Korbel was a **diplomat** from Czechoslovakia, a country in eastern Europe. Condoleezza was instantly fascinated with his class. The day she walked in he was discussing the Russian leader Joseph Stalin. Coldoleezza said later that she just fell in love with international **politics**. She wanted to learn everything she could about Russia, which was then called the Soviet Union.

As she did with everything else, Condoleezza threw herself into the study of Russia–the language, the people, the **culture**, everything. Korbel encouraged her to joined the University of Denver's school of international relations, which he had started. She made **political science** and the Soviet Union, her major courses of study.

Top student

Condoleezza graduated from the University of Denver with a bachelor's degree in international relations in 1974. She graduated with top honors and won the Political Science Honors Award. She was one of only 10 students recognized for outstanding work in the political science field. She also earned a place in Phi Beta Kappa, an organization for outstanding students. The Mortar Board, an honorary organization for senior women at the university, also welcomed her as a member. And she was named Outstanding Senior Woman. Nineteen-year-old Condoleezza Rice was the most honored woman in the University of Denver's class of 1974.

Condoleezza planned to continue her studies and get a master's degree at the University of Notre Dame in Indiana. This was her first time away from her parents. She spent a year at Notre Dame, earning a master's degree in government and international studies.

After getting her master's degree in August 1975, Condoleezza thought about going to law school. Korbel told her that she should become a professor instead of a lawyer. So she went back to the University of Denver to the Graduate School of International Studies but she wasn't sure what she wanted to do with her studies.

*When Rice stepped down from her post as **Provost** at Stanford, she was determined to refocus on her love of international politics and Russia in particular. "For me, visiting Russia is like breathing, "she has said.*

Chapter 3:
California, Here I Come

After graduating with a Ph.D in international studies, Rice, now 26 years old, received a fellowship to study in a one year program at Stanford University in California. At the end of the program, she would be a specialist in government security. She was the first female fellow ever to be admitted to the program.

Rice stayed at Stanford much longer than one year. After only a few months, she was asked to teach at the university. She became an assistant professor of political science at Stanford in the fall of 1981. As an African-American woman, Rice was a unique figure on campus. Most people in the political science department were white males.

Rice proved to be a demanding but exciting teacher. Her students thought she brought a great deal of passion to her classes and she encouraged heated debates. Rice usually opened her first lecture with something about football. She often compared the game of football to war.

Dr. Rice taught her students about international affairs, military strategies, and economics. The theme of many of her classes was power. Who has power in the world? Why do some countries have power and other countries do not? How should power be used? Her **political science** classes were popular because of her teaching methods. She challenged her students to do more than read books and listen to lectures. In class, they took on the roles of countries or leaders in the world. They had to think how those people would think. They had to act how those people would act. Dr. Rice used this method to help her students understand policies and news events from the inside out.

By 1984, Rice became one of Stanford's most respected professors. That year she won an award for excellence in teaching. She would later be awarded the School of Humanities and Sciences Dean's Award for Distinguished Teaching. Those are the two highest honors for the political science department at Stanford.

Youngest provost ever

In 1993 Rice became a full professor at Stanford. That same year she made national headlines when she became Stanford's provost, the person who manages the university's money. **Provost** is a very powerful job, second only in rank to the university president.

This image is a photo of Rice at Stanford. She has said, "Athletics gives you a kind of toughness and discipline that nothing else really does."

Stanford University is located in northern California. It opened its doors in 1891 and is named after its founders, Jane and Leland Stanford. The Stanfords established the university in memory of their son who died when he was 15 years old.

At Stanford, the **provost** is also responsible for the athletic department. Still a sports fanatic, this made Rice very happy. Rice was the first woman and the first African American to become provost at Stanford. At the age of 38, she was also the youngest provost in Stanford's 103-year history.

Stanford had been in financial trouble for a few years, and Rice's friends thought she was taking a miserable job. But Rice got right to work putting together a plan to get the school out of debt. Her plan made some people angry because they thought she was taking money away from programs for women and minority groups. Protests erupted all over campus. Finally, the U.S. government investigated Rice's plan. The investigation determined that no one was being treated unfairly. If Rice was bothered by all the fuss, she hid it well.

Rice's work as provost of Stanford University demanded a great deal of energy. But Condoleezza Rice knew just how she could fill up on energy again. As she had all of her life, she turned to music. Always striving to be better, she took piano lessons from a Stanford professor. She also joined a string quartet as a violinist. All four members of the quartet worked together at Stanford. They played music for their own entertainment. Along with her work, music and friendship filled Rice's Stanford years.

Condoleezza Rice's knowledge of Soviet affairs prepared her for meetings like this one with Russian Foreign Minister Igor Ivanov.

Chapter 4:
The Soviet Expert

While Rice was still at Stanford, she had the chance to meet Brent Scowcroft, one of President Ronald Regan's military **advisors**. He gave a lecture and Rice asked him some tough questions about the United States' relationship with other countries. Scowcroft was impressed.

In 1989, when George Herbet Walker Bush became President of the United States, he made Scowcroft his national security advisor. This meant that Scowcroft had to keep the president informed about what was happening in the world and how those things affected the safety of the United States. To do this well, Scowcroft needed his own team of experts. He asked Rice to leave Stanford to become his chief advisor on the Soviet Union. She accepted.

The end of the Cold War

Rice got to put her expertise to work almost as soon as she took the position. At the time, the United States (and the countries that supported it) and the Soviet Union (and the countries that supported it) were engaged in what was known as The Cold War. The two countries were not actually fighting, but there was a lot of distrust between them. The Soviet Union was a group of countries in Eastern Europe. They had a system of governement, called **Communism**, that the United States did not agree with. The United States worried that the Soviet Union would take control of other countries and spread Communism all over the world. The Soviet Union did not like the American **democratic** system of government, either. For 44 years, each nation did what it could to make sure the other did not become too powerful.

One of the major symbols of the Cold War was the Berlin Wall. The wall ran through the city of Berlin, Germany and separated Germany into two parts: East Germany and West Germany. East Germany had a Communist government and the support of the Soviet Union. West Germany had the support of the United States. Soldiers guarded the wall to make sure no one got across. Between 1961 (when the wall was built) and 1989, at least 80 people died trying to cross the wall.

In 1989 Communist goverments all over Europe were breaking down, thanks in part to friendly discussions between

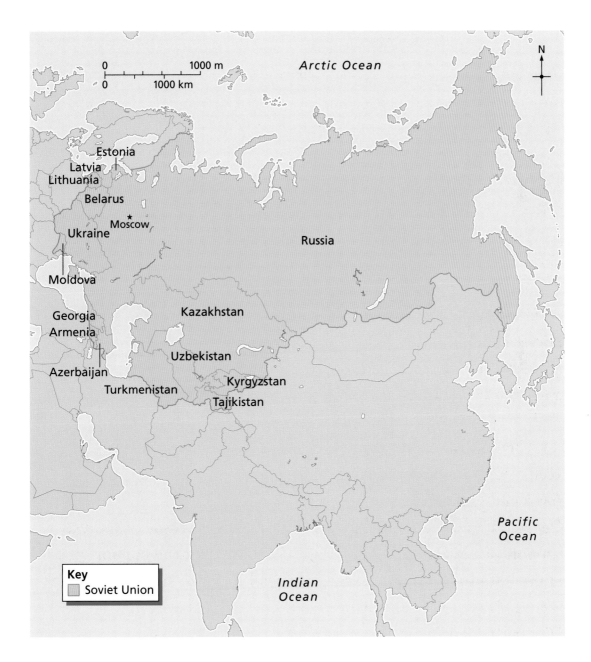

Key
Soviet Union

The Soviet Union (also called the Union of Soviet Socialist Republics or U.S.S.R.) was created in 1922 with four countries. By the time it fell apart in 1991, fifteen countries were part of the Soviet Union. They are all separate countries today.

The Berlin Wall came down in 1989.

President Regan and Mikhail Gorbechev, the leader of the Soviet Union. The Cold War between the United States and the Soviet Union was over.

But the Berlin Wall still stood. Then, in the fall of 1989, it was clear that the government in West Germany was falling apart. On November 9, the German people began tearing down the wall.

Rice worked with President Bush to create a plan for making Germany work as one country again. Her work was so impressive that later President Bush introduced Rice to Gorbechev, as the one who taught him everything he knows about the Soviet Union. In 1991, Germany was a whole nation once again.

The Gulf War

That same year, the United States entered in what was known as the Persian Gulf War. In 1990, Iraq, a small country in the Middle East, had taken control of Kuwait, a neighborning country. In 1991, when it appeared that Iraq was going to try to take over Saudi Arabia next, the United States stepped in. Saudi Arabia was an ally of the United States. Iraq was not.

By this time, the Soviet Union no longer existed. The countries that were once part of the Soviet Union were now independent countries. Russia was the largest and most powerful of the countries that were once the Soviet Union. Now that the Cold War

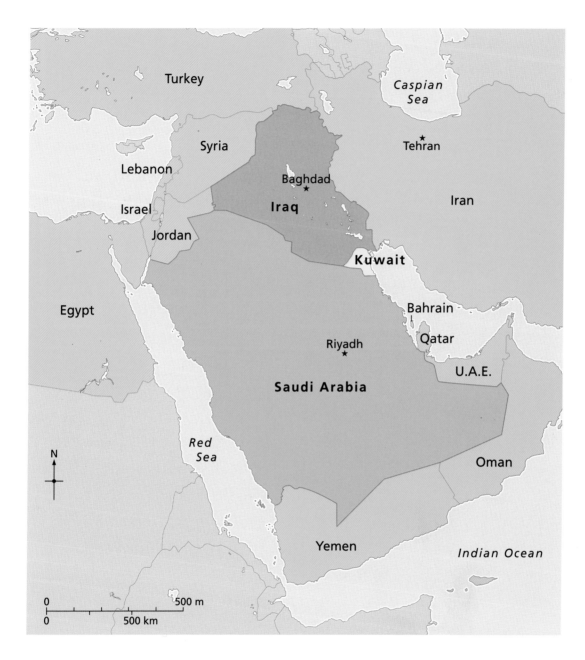

This map of the Middle East shows Iraq, Kuwait, and Saudi Arabia, where the Persian Gulf War took place.

was over, the United States could ask Russia for help in the Gulf War. To make this happen, Rice attended three **summits** with Russian president Gorbachev.

Leaving Washington

While Rice found her work with the government exciting, she missed teaching. At the end of 1991, she returned to Stanford. She also worked as an advisor for several major companies. She had a very impressive reputation now, and these major companies knew that being linked to Condoleezza Rice would make them seem impressive, too.

One of the companies Rice worked with was Chevron Corporation, a company that handles oil. She worked on several projects where her knowledge of Russia was very useful. She even had an oil tanker named after her, the *SS Condoleezza Rice*.

This photo of (from left to right) Condoleezza Rice, Vice President Richard Cheney, President George W. Bush, Secretary of Defense Donald Rumsfeld, First Dog, Barney, and Gen. Richard Myers was taken at Persident Bush's ranch in Crawford, Texas.

Chapter 5:
A New Breed of Republican

While working with President George H. W. Bush in the late 1980s and early 1990s, Rice got to know the Bush family, including the president's son George W. Bush. George W. Bush was impressed with Rice's knowledge of international relations, but their mutual love of sports made them friends.

In 2002, when George W. Bush ran for president, he wanted Rice to be part of his campaign team. She left Stanford to become Bush's **foreign affairs advisor**. This meant that she had to help Bush create a plan for dealing with other nations. It also meant answering tough questions from reporters. Rice loved being part of Bush's campaign. No matter how difficult a reporter's question, she never appeared to be flustered or unsure.

George W. Bush won the presidential election in 2000. As soon as he was declared the winner, he began to choose the people who would help him do his job. One of these people is the National Security Advisor. Bush appointed Rice to this position.

The National Security Advisor is part of a larger team called the **National Security Council** (NSC). This group was first created in 1947 by President Truman. He needed a team to help him decide how to best keep the United States safe. The NSC is made up of the National Security Advisor, the Vice President, the Secretary of State, the Secretary of Defense, and the Secretary of the Treasury. It was Rice's responsibility to gather the opinions of the council members and simplify them for the president.

September 11, 2001

On a typical day, Rice wakes up at ten minutes before five in the morning and works out on her treadmill. Rice is usually in her office—which is right down the hall from the president's—by 6:30 a.m., and sometimes does not leave until after 9 p.m. On September 11, 2001, she was at her desk at her usual time. Shortly before 9 a.m., her assistant rushed into her office with startling news. An American Airlines flight from Boston, Massachusetts, had just crashed into the north tower of the World Trade Center in New York City. Like many Americans, Rice thought the crash was a terrible accident. However, within minutes, Rice learned that another flight from Boston had crashed into the World Trade Center's South Tower. Immediately, she knew it was a terrorist attack.

As National Security Advisor Rice was responsible for briefing the press.

Before 10 a.m., Rice learned that a third plane had crashed. This time it hit the Pentagon building in Washington, D.C. About 10 minutes later, there was news of a fourth plane crashing, this one in Pennsylvania. Soon she heard the frightening news that the Twin Towers had fallen.

Like other members of the White House staff, Rice was immediately ordered to go to an underground **bunker** where she would be safe. But before she left, she called the president. He was visiting a school in Sarasota, Florida, at the time. She advised that he should not return to Washington right away. She and others in the administration believed that another attack on Washington, D.C. might be coming.

When Rice got to the bunker, Vice President Richard Cheney was there. She immediately placed calls to leaders around the world to tell them that the U.S. government was still operating. Then she set up meetings with the President and the **National Security Council**. In the meantime, President Bush was on Air Force One, on his way to a safe place. Rice and the Vice President kept in contact with Bush while he was in the air.

Before September 11, not many people outside Washington, D.C. or Stanford were very familiar with Rice. But after September 11, most of the world recognized her. Every time the president

These two beams of light shine where the World Trade Center towers once stood. The lights are a way for the city of New York to honor the people who died in the terrorist attacks of September 11, 2001.

Osama bin Laden is on the Federal Bureau of Investigation (FBI) Ten Most Wanted list. Bin Laden is believed to be responsible for the attacks on September 11.

appeared on television with news related to the attack, Rice was at his side. As always, she was calm and steady under pressure.

Investigators found evidence that a terrorist named Osama bin Laden had planned the September 11th attacks. Bin Laden was living in a country in Asia called Afghanistan. He was being protected by a very powerful group called the Taliban. President Bush was determined to find bin Laden and bring him to justice for attacking the United States. Bush sent several thousand U.S. troops to Afghanistan in November of 2001. The United States was at war.

The war in Afghanistan was part of what President Bush called the "war on terror." It was the Bush administration's effort to destroy terrorism all over the world. During this time, Rice was on the phone every morning at 7, talking to Secretary of State Colin Powell and Secretary of Defense Donald Rumsfeld. These men were in charge of making the military plans for the war on terror. It was Rice's responsibility to share the key points of their reports with the president.

In March 2003, President Bush declared war on a small country in the Middle East called Iraq. Bush believed that the leader of Iraq, Saddam Hussein, was a serious threat to the United States. Rice was at the president's side whenever he spoke to the American people about this new war.

Condoleezza Rice testified before the 9/11 Comission on April 8, 2004.

Defending the president

After the nation had time to heal from the attacks of September 11 and think about what had happened, people began to ask questions. Could anything have been done to prevent the attacks? Whose fault was it that the United States had not been protected? What could be done to make sure such attacks never happen again? In 2004, a committee called the 9/11 Comission was formed to answer some of these questions.

The 9/11 Commission questioned many government officials, including President Bush and Condoleezza Rice. Rice was calm and collected when she answered the committee's questions. She wanted the committee and the American people watching her on television to know that there was nothing the United States government could have done to prevent the September 11th attacks. "Had we thought that there was an attack coming on Washington (D.C.), or New York," she said during her testimony, "we would have moved heaven and Earth to try and stop it."

Rice has had to defend Bush in other areas as well. When people question the war on terror, she explains that she believes the United States is fighting the war in the best possible way. She is a **steadfast** supporter of the president, and helps make sure his views are understood by the American people.

Secretary of State Condoleezza Rice is known for her charm and her intelligence.

Chapter 6:
The Steel Magnolia

Rice's friends say she is a "steel magnolia" because of her blend of strength, intelligence, and supreme confidence, and her southern charm. They also say that her life is her work. She is totally devoted to her position in the president's cabinet.

Indeed, it does seem that most of her time is spent on the job. But when she leaves the office for the day, she goes to her apartment on the Potomac River, where she still has the grand piano her parents bought for her when she was thirteen. She has little time for playing, but sometimes when a few friends are visiting, she gives an informal performance.

In 2002, however, Rice gave a piano performance that would have made her mother proud. At an awards dinner in Washington, D.C., Rice performed a duet with world-famous cellist Yo-Yo Ma.

Condoleezza Rice performing with cellist Yo Yo Ma.

While she doesn't always have much time for a social life, Rice always finds time to honor her religious beliefs. Religion is a very important part of Rice's life and has carried her through difficult times, including the deaths of both parents. Her mother died of cancer in 1985. Her father had a heart attack in 2000, and she spent as much time as possible at his side while she worked on Bush's election campaign. He lived just long enough to see his daughter become National Security **Advisor**.

Diplomat to the world

In November 2004, George W. Bush was elected to serve a second term as president of the United States. General Colin Powell was Secretary of State during President Bush's first four years. Now General Powell wanted to retire. President Bush chose Condoleezza Rice to be the new Secretary of State.

The Secretary of State is an important position in the White House. This person gives advice to the president on relationships between the United States and other countries around the world. The Secretary of State travels frequently to represent the United States and to meet with leaders of other nations.

Dr. Rice is only the second woman ever to serve as Secretary of State and the first African-American woman.

When Rice left Stanford in 1999, she was asked whether she would consider working in Washington, D.C. again. She replied, "Oh, maybe. Washington was great fun—1989 to 1991 was really a super time. I'll cross that bridge when I get to it, but I'm not just dying to go."

Rice still loves football, and she watches the games whenever she can. She once said that if it were not for football, she would have had time to publish many more books. Rice's first book was published in 1984.

In 2004, *Forbes* magazine named Rice the most powerful woman in the world. Rice doesn't like to think too much about what her future holds, but no matter what, there's always the National Football League.

In Her Own Words

"[My] parents had me absolutely convinced that, well, you may not be able to have a hamburger at Woolworth's but you can be president of the United States." — *Condoleezza Rice about overcoming the effects of racism.*

Glossary

advisor one who gives information to another, such as on legal or political matters

ambassador official government agent sent to another country

budget amount of money that can be spent for various purposes

bunker fortified chamber usually below ground

civil rights personal liberty rights guaranteed to U.S. citizens by the Constitution

communist member of a government system in which a single party controls the state-owned means of production

culture beliefs, social forms, and material characteristics of a particular group

democratic having to do with a government of the people

demonstration public display of group feelings about a person or cause, as civil rights

diplomat one who is skilled in handling affairs among nations

fluent to be well versed in something, such as fluent in speaking Spanish

foreign affairs matters having to do with relationships between governments

integrated not divided by race

intellectual person given to study and creative use of the mind

liberal one who favors a political party that is not bound by tradition

National Security Council agency of U.S. government that advises the president on domestic, foreign, and policies

political science area of study concerned mainly with government institutions

politics art or science of influencing government policy

provost high-ranking university officer

racism belief that racial differences make one race superior to another

segregated divided according to race, such as schools for blacks and schools for whites

steadfast firmly fixed in place

summit meeting of highest government officials

Timeline

1954 Condoleezza Rice is born November 14, Birmingham, Alabama.

1958 Condoleezza plays piano in public for the first time.

1963 Racists bomb Baptist church in Birmingham; Condoleezza's friend is killed.

1964 On family trip to Washington, D.C., Condoleezza decides she will be in the White House one day.

1965 The Rice family moves to Tuscaloosa, Alabama.

1968 The Rice family moves to Denver, Colorado; Condoleezza enters St. Mary's Academy, an integrated school.

1970 Rice graduates from St. Mary's, enters University of Denver; meets Josef Korbel, becomes interested in politics.

1974 Rice graduates from University of Denver with a degree in international Relations.

1975 Rice earns master's degree from Notre Dame, enters University of Denver Graduate School of International Studies.

1981 Rice earns Ph.D., August; takes teaching post at Center for International Security and Arms Control, Stanford University.

1987 Rice is named associate professor at Stanford, becomes provost, youngest to hold job in school's history; meets Brent Scowcroft, advisor to President George Bush.

1989 Rice takes leave of absence, joins National Security Council of George Bush.

1991 Rice returns to Stanford, serves on boards of U.S. corporations.

2000 Rice leaves Stanford to join campaign of George W. Bush, becomes his national security advisor after election.

2005 President Bush appoints Rice to be Secretary of State.

Further Information

Further reading

Bowdish, Lynea. *With Courage: Seven Women Who Changed America.*
New York: Mondo, 2004.

Burke, Rich. *George W. Bush.* Chicago: Heineman, 2003.

Naden, Corrine J. and Rose Blue. *The Importance of George W. Bush.*
San Diego: Lucent, 2004.

Ryan, Bernard Jr. *Condoleezza Rice, National Security Advisor and
Musician.* New York: Ferguson, 2004.

Wade, Mary Dodson. *Condoleezza Rice: Being the Best.* Brookfield,
CT: Millbrook, 2003.

Address

Dr. Condoleezza Rice
The U.S. State Department
2201 C Street NW
Washington, D.C. 20520
www.state.gov

Index